A Windmill Near Calvary

A Windmil

Near Calvary

by Keith Waldrop

"You want too much."—a friend

Ann Arbor

The University of Michigan Press

Copyright © by The University of Michigan 1968
All rights reserved
Library of Congress Catalog Card No. 68–29265
Published in the United States of America by
The University of Michigan Press and simultaneously
in Rexdale, Canada, by Ambassador Books Limited
United Kingdom agent: The Cresset Press
Manufactured in the United States of America

Some of these poems have appeared in the
following publications: *Wayne Review,*
The Wolgamot Interstice, Paris Review,
Open Places, Keith Tank Line, The New
Yorker: "Conversion," copyright 1968 by
The New Yorker Magazine. "After Birth" was
a Perishable Press broadside. "To The Sincere
Reader" is the text for a volume of collage-
drawings by Nelson Howe. The French text
of Queneau's "Je crains pas ça tellment" is in
his collection *L'instant fatal* (copyright 1948
by Librairie Gallimard).

for Rosmarie

Contents

After Birth

"through a beginning, that is, fear, God created heaven and earth."—*The Zohar*

My features were formed in a woman's
womb. My face glistened
while I waded in another world
unwilling to touch land. Dead horses,
lining the road, mark the way home.
Sugar feeds her veins and her bladder fills
with crystals. Mother, I see you
young, standing in a tree or sitting
by a staircase labeled *ICE,* waiting
to try the slipper on. But in the bowels
cells grow savage, tribes without law. Unarmed
around or underneath.
Brother Allen drives a big black car
(I took my cancer to church in a jar)
Brother Allen preaches the world will end in ash
And sends twelve ushers into the aisles for cash
Brother Allen speaks in tongues and Brother Allen interprets
(His serpent gobbles up all the other serpents)
From Miracle Valley to Hot Springs
The lame leap up the dumb tongue sings
And those who know their names are sealed
Flop in the sawdust shouting "Healed we're healed"
Withdrawn
(Lord if Thou hadst been here, or I where you were,
I would not now suffer)
O rose des vents
All sewers flow into the earth and
the earth is full and running over.
My black double is defined by moonlight
on the snow. Two wires strung overhead
make sled tracks that will disappear
and reappear. You were always married, Mother,

and you never had a husband. Old
women grow fierce sometimes. Their eyes flash,
hardening. They find nothing good to look at
except what shines out of the dark.
Cats' eyes turn into discarded beer cans.
We have all listened to
unknown tongues, and I have pretended
to translate. Poets wear a veil
to hide their empty sockets. Between and back
behind the eyes is the dwelling place of light.
The bag of bone is death. Stiffnecked dust
had to breed a worm to feed the worms.
For a fifth time, with a second mistake.
Did you tremble at that last gasp of an
old man's lust? Those who should know
claim that when God began to create, he created
a single point.

Angel to Love, Man to World

I was reared among prophets, who saw
one true Word in a deceiving world and
fixed their gaze on it. I remember (dimly)
stunning silences, and messages—come down
whole from above—and mysteries, in a matrix
like gnashing of teeth.

Now what possesses me? Someone who didn't
know me might take me for a connoisseur—
I stare till I wonder those canvases (for
instance) are not consumed, and expect any day
to see it posted: *défense de manger
les objets d'art.*

It's simple voracity, the garden-of-Eden
chomp. (We see—by and large—what
we want to see. At least that explains
why just looking around us makes us
guilty—by breathing open Adam's eyelid God
damned the mud.)

A shamed child would like, as Erikson
puts it, "to destroy the eyes of the world."
Failing that, he closes his own eyes, tightly.
As for me, I cultivate my field of nothingness
a bit extravagantly. (I know the world exists.
I do not know

how the world exists. I do not know how
I know the world exists. Empty mind
is a greedy darkness. Brightness is
all there is. From a bright point
light pulsates, throb after throb, into the
ravening dark.)

If my retinal sensitivity were increased, I
would perceive, I'm told, not more occult *mysterious*
hills or finer prospects, but irregularities
of the light itself. Strange as it
seems, there's nothing more to see.
(Fabulous world.)

No one thing will do—more and more, nothing
will substitute for anything else. Wrapped
in the accidents of an untasted
apple, even Good and Evil might be appetizing.
And couldn't I regard my death as Eve did hers—
salivating?

I'd like an inclusive mind, where nothing could
possibly be out of the question. Like Saint
Mark's facade where, half way up a
clutter of Christianity and Venetian lace, are
four Roman horses, poised, in place.
Surely it was

thinking like this made Brueghel paint
a windmill near Calvary. When Adam, as it
fell out, got too old to know Eve, he sat
his inspired carcase down by his hoe, watching
his sweaty children screw up generation
after generation.

Antiquary

One who collects objects of great age.

Some people try, before cashing in, to make
their lives into shrines. Mine seems to be turning out,
as predicted, a small provincial museum, the kind
that might have in some corner or other one work
you could be interested in, if you knew it was there.
Memorials and keepsakes hang around, half catalogued. Some
curiosa, here and there a whopper—who else
could maintain a scarlet nose drinking
Dr. Pepper? I have my precedents. Lots of men
shuffle off, leaving a ball of tinfoil too large to get
out of the attic or half a century of the New York Times
or some other mess. I keep everything. Old
gods and old ads fade together; both
show better on a neutral wall. Philosophies, old hat,
catch dust on a rack. The trouble is
I'm a glutton. The floor is cluttered,
the shelves go across the windows. I trip
sometimes over ancient arguments or
a lid I can't place, or claim two different heads
to be Saint Thomas's. Nothing, nothing will I
surrender. There is little enough as it is.
I may, of course, croak tomorrow, stumbling
from the larder, but I will not set
my house in order.

Beauty

According to a newspaper account, maybe distorted
in my remembering (told me, come to think of it, by my
brother, who sometimes lies), a man carrying a shotgun
down Main Street in some town or other
explained to a policeman that an hour before, on the
same block, another man, a *total stranger,*
spit in his eye and told him it was raining. It is
possible to look, neither at surfaces nor beneath them,
but geometrically, squinting slightly to accommodate
things to our net of vision, robbing raw objects
of their atrocity. The only danger being that
the whole world may convert and you be left
with nothing but the music of, say,
(if you're lucky) Mozart or (if you aren't) Liszt.
A formidable danger. Still,
beauty is nothing to sneeze at.

Before Bed

"what shall we do for our sister?"—*Cant.* 8:8

Girls with fat thighs and no breasts
stare at the daughters of television.
All they know bound into that bright box,
they cannot tell bay leaves from
savory. They are learning what they will
never understand. Their mothers
packed every little hope into a cedar chest,
more than a man could carry. They watch,
uncomprehending, diaphanous movements in snow.
If they hope, they hope for a ring of
cheap music and boobies like mountains,
no other dream worth sleeping for.

Conversion

I am already sweeping towards my most
permanent state. Keith means "wind," according
to *What to Name the Baby*. There is
a paradise promised for those who despise
whatever turns—flesh going sour—and I
have despised it.

But I have been converted. Stock dreams can be
flicked on, the assured voice forming first and
then, slowly, its radiant body, but they fulfill
no wish of mine. All my aerier hopes
have dwindled to a momentary point of light,
disappearing.

Reality is what does not change, i.e., reality
is what does not exist, held desperately.
All my past sins I attribute to a
commerce with angels, someone else's. The
earth brings forth of itself and the rest is only
worth a thought.

Now faces crop out of the most random
inorganic patterns, usually nobody's in particular
—I take them as a less specific, less
beautiful, Allegory of Spring. Sometimes,
at night, my head swerves in a rising spiral
of labyrinthine

vertigo, descending only in the arc of sleep.
But I have learned to like the dust I am fed by
winds that shift across an actual world.
I am already what I will be later. And the cycles
shorten. I owe letters to so many, I doubt
that I will ever catch up now.

Creamery Road

I hear from probably a mile away
(sounds carry across these hills) human
voices, but the words are indistinct.
Even the smell of a skunk
is pleasant, if distant enough.

Credo

It is a great doctrine that says we
believe as much as we deserve. Saint Thomas was worth,
apparently, everything in the *Summa,* though he couldn't
    stomach
the Immaculate Conception. Mrs. Katache of Arkhangelsk
supposes she's a chamber pot and shrieks to be emptied.
What does one have to do, or be, to accept
streets of gold or the big lift at the Rapture? Perhaps
Gregory, for his compassion, was allowed to imagine sinners
scorching out their stains in Purgatory.
I know a Christian, says she
just has to laugh thinking of all those atheists going to
wake up in hell. There are those for whom God is
dead, but who fear the Devil or my black cat. I think
the time is coming and maybe now is when the tree that
overshadows this house will grow from my forehead, spreading
like veins, ring after ring.

Essay

for Dorothy Charles

At least one poet [Traherne] thanked the Lord for giving him
desire, in a general sense of course. For a time
one of my brothers slept eighteen hours a day, having
nothing to rise for. Leonardo thought the world would end
by a gradual diminution of desire, in, obviously,
the narrower sense. It seems to me little Polly
Morfus usually trades in her perversity on a passionless
propriety. The farther our desire extends, the more we know of
the void. *This is a true story:* Two girls, respectable,
both Catholic to a fault, on some wild impulse picked
up two old friends, men, by a mysteriously vague
invitation. They took them to an apartment they knew was
empty for the night and, still on impulse, while the
tension mounted, began acting provocative, a bit crude.
They even, I think, got into robes and served some wine.
All mysteriously, as if there were a secret plan.
The men got more and more uncomfortable. You understand
they knew these girls and must have been convinced something
would happen to stop this incredible scene. What *could* happen?
They all started beating the hell out of each other
with pillows or cushions or whatever was handy. They were
beautiful girls. The one who told me all this didn't
understand it and was a little ashamed that after this
they left the apartment disheveled, with feathers strewn and
furniture overturned and a light burning.

Euphrates

The air, strained, whistles through cracks
and roars in the woods across the road.
The relative humidity is rising and tonight
it will rain. I have a spider in my labyrinth,
some dog turning my garbage pail over,
un chat pissant parmi les livres. Genesis
says before there was even light the wind howled
over chaos, everything slopped together,
bark and bones oozy with petroleum or
cod-liver oil, all flow and no membrane, only
a little tense at the surface. I dialed the
weather bureau and a nice girl on a record
said, "All flesh is grass." The crackling net,
punky with thunder, cannot hold the flood
or continue to divide the upper waters from the lower.

Festival de Musique
chez le Marquis de Sade

Sheep that wore untuned bells
are disemboweled for viols

Cherry limbs are first
chopped then polished and pierced

and lungs fired by the sun
that fattens Provençal wine

pump fouled air through
the still staves of Rameau

Shape is dealt by the rod
and only the shape is dead

festival de musique
chez le Marquis de Sade

For Two Different Deaths

I. Of S., Killed on a Freeway

He was probably sloppy drunk. I think he hated
concrete. I hardly knew him and couldn't quite take
his gushings on friendship. He probably
hated us all on occasion, figuring us
cowards not to be dissolved with him. And we were.
One has to draw the line somewhere. Mostly he hated
himself, I've no idea why. His stomach
was not rigid enough for academic life.
He cried like a baby when Jeffers died,
and for Marilyn Monroe.
Perhaps it was not enough merely to see and know
that great vans across the median can crush.
I do not think he ever professed to believe
the text that guarantees the elements will melt.

II.   *To Jackie: an Admiration*

Nobody knew how to talk to you—you
so rarely answered. I can only write to you
with the old formulas (you are not the
only lovely one who ever died before
her time).

So now I write to you this way ("you") —
a convention whose rules are crazy enough
to allow me to write to you. You
hated conventions, but could not bear to
be alone.

You plunked low C on the harpsichord half
the night one night, while Mary smashed beer bottles
on the bedroom wall and a Japanese sculptor tried
to choke a friend because she suggested he ought to show
in New York.

If I could arrange, in simple chronology,
photos of you—at sixteen, eighteen, twenty . . . —
and beside them number the years (I do not
know exactly how old you were), it would mean (have
meant) nothing to you.

You rot with the rest of the dead—"you" do
not exist—and, caring nothing at all, care little less now
than you did (single-minded, you were an almost
private language) what we do with our
words.

For Zhenia

"The numinous is essentially the luminous."—Edwyn Bevan

You have seen passing through the store
slow burners moldering slowly or

Outdoors the sudden decay of sun
trash burning in a world of ash

You have felt your human weight
decomposing into sentient heat

And know in the vacuum black no mystery
that might break down to light

From Malherbe:
"Jeanne, tandis que tu fus belle"

Jeannie, while you had looks, you
Were beautiful without a peer;
And now that Annie's day is here
There's no one to compare her to.
I know a few years will have scarred
Her forehead, just as yours is marred;
And her hair, curling blonde and fresh,
Will be outraged as your curls were.
But there we are, the way of all flesh:
I wanted you, and I want her.

From Raymond Queneau:
"Je crains pas ça tellment"

That don't scare me so much death of my guts
death of my bones death of my nose
That don't scare me so much me a skeeter sort
baptized Raymond from a line of Queneaus

That don't scare me so much where my books get stacked
in book stalls in johns in dust and doldrums
That don't scare me so much me who scribble a pack
and boil down death into some poems

That don't scare me so much Soft night flows
between ringwormy eyelids over dead eyeballs
Night is soft a redhead's kiss
honey of meridians at north and south poles

I'm not scared of that night not scared of absolute
sleep It must be heavy as lead
dry as lava dark as the sky
deaf as a beggar bellowing on a bridge

I'm scared stiff of unhappiness crying pain
and dread and rotten luck and parting too long
I'm scared of the lardbellied abyss that holds sickness
and time and space and the mind gone wrong

But I'm not so scared of that lugubrious imbecile
who'll come and spit me on his toothpick point
when I'm down and with eyes vague and placid I'll
have lost my cool to the collecting rats

Someday I'll sing Ulysses or maybe Achilles
Aeneas or maybe Dido Quixote maybe Sancho
Someday I'll sing pleasures the idle know
the fun of fishing or the peace of villas

All fagged out today by the hours as they wind out
trudging like an old nag around the dial
a thousand pardons from this skull—a ball—
for doling out plaintively this song of the void

From The Loeb:
Paulus Silentiarius, *Pal. Anth.* V: 230

With one yellow hair
Doris tied my wrists
Proclaiming me prisoner
And I laughed at first

Thinking that yoke light
Till I tried to go
And found I could not break it
Then I bellowed

Like a slave in irons
And now I dangle
By a hair wherever she deigns
To drag me.

From The Loeb And Elsewhere:
Pal. Anth. VII: 621

I, Sophocles [we do not
know who this
Sophocles was],
went down to Hades
laughing,
because I ate Sardinian
celery
[a poisonous herb, *Ranunculus
sardous,* whose
bitter taste could draw
the lips back in a
grin or sarcastic snarl, *sardonic,*
like a dog's]. So I
died, and
others
otherwise, but all in one
way or another.

From the Porch

Whoever turns that corner at the
end of the street
disappears behind a
brick wall, out of my sight and out of
my world. It quiets me to think of this, as
Mrs. Pratt's awkward ass veers past and into broad
perspective and proceeds,
diminishing.

Frozen Water

I would run downtown for a drink, if I
drank, and if the snow were not drifted
in my driveway—and still coming down, coming
sideways in fact, dry, light, windswept.

Furniture

I have come a long way, and the long way
round. And I have collected some
furniture: a movie-house chair, an organ
pipe, a Tibetan prayer horn, ten thousand books or nearly.
And I have avoided—so far—mumps, clap, and
manual labor. And probably I have never liked anything
enough. But everything may change; and everything will
come to nothing. There was a woman once who bathed in blood
to save her skin. It didn't help. Nothing helps.
Casanova lost his touch. The whole globe groans
as if there were some other travail and I am
delirious (= out of the rut) but towards what egress? to what
issue? Where I used to live, the local Fire Chief
burnt himself up, smoking in bed. Such a waste of motive.
Rank and lovely our best joy, Rosmarie; the damp soul
beats time best. The house I was born in had an
oval pane in the door. Oh yes—and we have (still)
a fat black cat, who sucked eggs when he was a kitten
and now has one dull fang. He will die one of
these days, probably out of sight, in some crevice.

Graven Images

In my neighborhood, even the children
are travelers. The kids I wave to,
because they wait for the school bus
in front of my house, have
some of them lived in three states.
At least one was born in California.

And this is Connecticut, where—I was
warned—a man is a stranger
unless his grandfather is buried here, and
shiftless if his house was not
inherited. Nevertheless, the new over-
hang across the street is posted *For Sale*.

And in graveyards around this Durham,
whose perpetual care lapsed ages ago,
bones borne in wooden boats from Old England
lie packed in plots of rocky dirt,
remembered by slate or granite
slabs that boast a coffin blossoming

or the Archangel with his trumpet or,
oftener, Time snuffing out a candle
or a skeleton or just a simple skull.
Some brat has chalked the word *screw*
at the edge of my drive, and doodled
around it unequivocal hieroglyphics.

Green Sickness

Jack Crack
took his palette to Paris
and writing his friends
"Enfin! j'ai trouvé mon propre style"
painted again and again the same picture,
as if a pregnancy
could be indefinitely prolonged.

Helen

for Bente

"That story is not true.
You never sailed in the benched ships.
You never went to the city of Troy."
     —Stesichorus (trans. Lattimore)

What Stesichorus failed to say (blinded
poet reworking a blind poet's story to
get back his eyes) is that Helen, hidden
in Egyptian mysteries, nevertheless knew
all that passed in Sparta, Cyprus, Sidon,
Troy: the benched ships, the towers, Paris.

Who itched to finger her phantom (for which
two continents met on a clattering battleground and
left it cluttered with dead men) she perceived,
coldly I suppose: Achilles' snatched
glance from below, Priam's impotent fumbling,
the arms and legs and prick of Paris.

Paris knew nothing (for giving a prize
to the goddess who promised most) except
a simulacrum fevering him, until Troy caught fire.
All I mean, Bente, is that every beautiful woman
causes war, a sorrow of theft or annihilation,
and the chariots smash in a field where no blade moves

Horror Story

I had two
grandfathers. One was a bald gentle postmaster
in Leeton, Missouri; he died and was buried.
The other was some kind of preacher;
I never saw him. The terrible thing about
ghosts is that we know they are not there.
Two grandmothers. One chased me with a
broom because I accused her of riding it.
The other stopped listening and went deaf.
They both survived their husbands, but
now they are both dead. My father is
dead too, but this is no elegy.
I was disappointed early, by lack of precision.
I found it hard to keep a grip
on outlines. They always slip.
The fine delineation swells
around the edges, where it smells.
Woman, be strange, take me with your eyelid.
Nothing in dead landscapes suggests terror.
I have married a wife whose
surface I adore. And other surfaces.
Who knows what may leap out from the shadows?
Loved houses are haunted. And I have
no explanation.

In Lieu of an Alba

Don't worry, Patricia,
about being forgotten:
you have left stray hairs
around, like a shedding cat;
even years from now
we will be pulling them off our suits
or gagging because they lodge
back of the tongue.

Libido

The girls who use the pay phones in the
corner drugstore are
desperate. I put my foot down
heavy and go eighty. The first
man, someone says, fell in the
muck and God, rather than clean him up,
turned him inside out. On a mountaintop
a doomed daughter beats her unpressed teats
and wails bitterly. Four days a year
I make a ceremony of standing
still and listening hard to
the frigging wind.

Lunch

The table is loaded. I marvel at my
appetite. I wonder if the void I stuff
is symbolic. At sixteen I considered
suicide and decided against it, on
purely hedonistic grounds. In his last days
my father got overweight, living alone, on
lima beans and schnapps. My brother Julian was
reduced at Leavenworth but now he lets his belly
hang out of his shirt as he feeds steaks to his
cat and laughs at the bulging globe. The Marquis de Sade, too,
eventually ate himself obese, while training lunatics
to act out in public his very personal complexes.
I marvel at all great appetites: Doctor Johnson,
Thomas Aquinas, Wolgamot. Food is Brahman, the text says,
and I suppose the devil, then, is the stuff
I void. People have eaten themselves to death,
and now, here, at this loaded table, it's hard to remember
how for a long time they had to coax and even force me
to open my mouth to the few things I disliked less
than the rest; it is hard now to imagine
such connoisseurship.

Meditation

Styles change. Some speak in tongues now
who would not hear of it a few years ago.
Articulate hallelujahs gone back in the throat somewhere.
I wonder if Kenneth Pike has discussed this problem.
In Central, South Carolina, tongues were worlds of iniquity;
at Greenville, too, where Bob Jones, Jr., intoned *Now is the
winter of our discontent* to a congregation not so sure
that was the will of God. God spoke to Elijah as a
still small voice, to Job from the whirlwind, to Moses from a
   shrub.
Styles change. We get Doc Bill's platitudes. (Christ!)
How much noise can we stand? Everywhere I hear pianos
being smashed. In the Black Room there is silence. No one can
   take
that much more than three days. Some advanced yogins try
to concentrate on ether.
Socrates, coming to die, said
Pull yourselves together.
But there's nothing to pull, only bats are in the belfry. The baby
babbles to hear himself and at the end of ourselves we scream
or bay at the moon. When Earl Prahl sings, his monkeys
go into withdrawal symptoms. And after all, there's so little
to say, the style's what really matters. And if God
could be conceived as having the energy to talk, he just might
jerk the syllables back into his throat and gargle forth
uncontrollably the unspeakable.

Metal Fatigue

When I drive I get sleepy, especially
on the Turnpike, where the only stops
are to pay toll, get gas, or garbage up. My image
of the car is a glossy metal, fluid,
not so much moving as extending, under pressure, from New
York to Washington, arterial. The Empire State Building
after a certain number of vibrations, tired
of being played on, will lie down along
Fifth Avenue. It's bound to happen. I am
roused for the moment by the distressing message
that my tax dollars are at work.

Migraine

The perfect head hurts. Perhaps
because (someone said this) small as they are
too many thoughts can crowd and
crack the skull. Perhaps the greater
the surface of the brain, the more
opening for pain. Or do I
think I can exalt myself by
aching?—since I write "the *perfect* head."
But why now do I turn on myself, while
the weights lie on my temples?

Missing a Movie

Viridiana will be raped tonight, twice,
and I will not see it, and twice
those derelicts will pose for the flash
of their Last Supper. Fortunately
I have seen it already, blasphemous
apostolic crew, obscene Christ.

Sedentary tribes, peasants, clods,
settle for "protectors of the household,"
neither acquisitive nor adventurous—
universal deities are the product of
nomads: homeless people, homeless gods.

I sit in my study, lazy, busy, focused
because of a lamp that only incidentally
spills across a thousand spines. I must
forgo those thousand opportunities for
escape, and cannot attend her rape, being
behind, too far behind, and too hard pressed.

The lymph or plasma, the bloody fluid
that carries us, our *milieu intérieur,*
preserves us from the world as we walk through it,
from the "perpetual changes of external conditions," from
whatever cosmic influences there are.

Maybe it is not that I want to see her
(raped)—maybe what moves me is the thought
of the film's recurring, the images turned
over and over, twice there, tonight, and then
again, in theater after theater. In sleep, delta
rhythms, huge "waves of electrical flow,"

sweep overwhelmingly the brain's alleyways.
Synchronized, slow, they are the fellies
of the infernal wheel from which we scream
in dreams to be delivered. I would, if I had
time, stop and scrutinize each distraction.

Frame follows frame, and it is as if the picture
were moving, constantly, incorrigibly. No
divinity is worth his salt who cannot
when a thing is done undo it, or else
hold it still—keep it from fading until
it is just as if it had never happened.

Murder

"When in doubt have a man come through a
door with a gun in his hand."—Raymond Chandler

I have few enemies, considering my
personality (friends say I have no
values). Since there is nothing to do
I do complain, like Jephthah's daughter
crying not because she had to die but
because she was a virgin.

The lower classes are prone to murder
(Durkheim noticed that) while the upper favor
suicide—with nothing but blue above them,
their rage can only be noble, self-effacing.

The private eye in Chandler's novels is
a rude man, with the world at his ribs.
One good blow could finish him.
And a woman's face can be eaten away by water,
and a falling man is crushed because the
air fails to resist him.

Occult Physics

Since we see, clouding
the vacant room between, they
are unbroken motion

we know they are (1) alive
                and (2) in torment

On Measure

The delicate foot of
Phoebe Isolde Farmer
taps meters acceptable to, among others, the
   * * * *Poetry Journal* and the
University of * * *   * * * *Review* and to
her brother, a minister, who is paying
for the printing of a small
volume—while he should be
praying, "Lord, grant her
wings."

Past Mistress

My thoughts derive, I am certain, from an image
(clear, distinct) of you. At any rate
it is you, you in particular, I would
celebrate.

But like the memory of a hero, your legend
is confused by all the mechanisms of retrieval
and your name attached, arbitrarily, religiously, to a
story that's universal.

Forgive me if I think the wrong color to your eyes
or keep you improbably young. I suppose
we should not murmur, whatever pigeonholing time tries
on us, who took in each other such
ritual interest.

Pride of the House

If you want to know how Cuchulain looked
riding widdershins round the town in a battle-distortion
it took 3 × 50 naked maidens and three vats of ice water to
    temper,
look at the neighbor's cat Bootsy. His fur like nails,
his eyes turrets, fangs bared clean to the nostrils,
he cries like two sirens and attacks my broom till the
straw flies. We're all afraid of him.
His rage is wasted because I have interfered,
opening the screen for old Moby Dick, who adapts at once
to the house—food in his bowl, a cushion to curl up on.
He is content to accept, occasionally, our civilization.

Receivers

for Jocelyn

I knew a man who always locked his doors
for fear of thieves, and so he was lonely
all his life. By the fact that two images merge into one,
a wild-eyed philosopher surmised that the eyes *love*.
But what? If each other, they must cross and
be terribly frustrated focusing on the bridge of the nose.
The lucid rim, the cornea, perceives only pain.
Broken glass across the brick roadway, like crushed
ice, the clear cubes we used to wrap in a
towel and smash opaque with a hammer. Somebody's
windshield destroyed with a spider's design. For a few
moments only, the light can flash between us, O
delicate crystal.

Samsara

Uncle Charley (my granduncle),
after a life of startling promiscuity,
received a Christian burial.
And all the family
is certain he has gone to heaven
(because in his last years
he achieved a glandular serenity
and a look of loss).

Smart

We see whatever we learn to see. I am revised
with every new edition of *Gray's Anatomy*.
Even my blood resembles the models: red in the
arteries, blue in the veins. I am more and more
detailed. With every intelligent design, I
am drawn. Two little figures used to pull me
this way and that, till I found I was divided
I, over-I, It. Or a complicated trade with everyone I've
ever known. Or fields. It all makes sense. Lines run through
everything. Points are everywhere. Third-year physics students
sometimes cry because the world is—not invisible—
abstract. Uncertain as we are, we are certainly bombarded,
discontinuous, our reality flashes on and off like the sign for
Red's Rite Spot. The trouble is it *always* makes sense.
Even breaking down. The ball breaks the
balls. Those on the edge
scatter. These crashes
pierce my sockets. Dust
settles over dust
and ashes.
I keep my hands in my pockets.

A Spell

The house we live in is beginning to
sag. A new coat of charcoal gray hides
combustible siding, but inside, where we
live, the floorboards creak, send splinters through the
rug, the shelves hardly hold the books and the walls
barely hold up the shelves. It will not last.
Particularly right around the toilet: the linoleum
is eaten away, the wood rotting, and already we can see
light from the basement. Also the switches
sputter when a lamp goes on or off. Well, we will move.
Somebody else can take the trouble to repair
the plumbing and replaster. Or maybe they won't.
When this house was built, to keep the snow and mud off
someone's head and boots and shield his sex life from neighbors'
     evil
eyes, it must have aroused envy, if only
for being new. And, unlikely as it seems now, it was once
new. If a woman suffers great pain in labor
the Gypsies, who think lightning smells like garlic,
set fire to diseased wood, chanting
when the wood is gone
the pain is gone
when the wood is burnt
the pain is burnt away
while the wood goes
the pain goes

To Define Oblivion

"There are limits."—statement attributed to D. C. Hope

The void my nightmares chase away
stares at me in the glaring day.
Everybody's madness buzzes at the screen door.
I'll probably end up twitching,
with an unrestricted bladder. (That's not the least
of my worries, though it isn't the worst.)
The space at the hub, says the Tao, is more important
than the thirty spokes. Maybe the brain needs
empty pockets. When blood rides us like a destroyer,
then what we want's not just an erection
but the ensuing dereliction. Still,
it makes some difference how the clay is turned. Not just
any hole is worth poking around in. There
was a Werewolf, in days gone,
refused to put his trousers on
while anyone was watching, so embarrassing
it is to lay aside the beast and be man again.

To the Sincere Reader

My brother used to sell hot watermelons
to the citizens of Atlanta suburbs.
He claimed, of course, they were ice cold.
Diogenes, after spilling his seed beside his tub,
wished he could placate hunger by rubbing his belly.
I used to plant peach stones and cherry pits and
mark the place as one might mark a cat's grave.
Nothing edible ever came of it. There are fish
that swell up to frighten their enemies and some
explode when hauled into thin air. Black pips
fall in the ground and die. An intellectual Don Juan
I keep a list of all the books I've dipped into. *Festus*
sits bloated on the shelf, next to the complete poems
of Wordsworth. His immortality is doubtful, but his
one wild oat provides loaves for generations. I am
Mama Ubu with a swollen world to carry. Be careful.
Whatever I look upon is digested. Whoever hears me
is digested. The axe that enters my lungs is digested
suddenly. With my raw hands I scoop out the red
meat, seeds and all. And I carry also my grave
within me and it plummets, rounded like a teardrop.

Towards a Final, 10 Dec. 1963

for James Camp

On the last day I am thirty,
cars stand in slush
along the expressway to Detroit, drivers
gunning useless horses
that have the strength but not the skill
to fly.
An hour separates River Rouge
and Wayne University. Flags stand
at half-mast. I have seen, I swear,
tumbleweed roll down Woodward. I once thought
the Lord would come, in clouds of the air,
to Emporia, Kansas. Now, on the last day
I am thirty, I think the clouds will drop
more slush, the expressway stalled, filled up, wild engines
straining, pounding out gases that smell like Detroit,
while the sun shafts the clouds and flakes of grease
fall. My German car
is cold but watertight, and if its motor
fails, it may still float. I must
examine my few hopes before these clotted lines
disperse enough to merge
onto Cass or Woodward.

49

A Web

Count Dracula found it hard to die, there was
so much blood around. I sometimes dredge for
immortality, among the second-hand book shops, and elsewhere.
Something succulent, what else could tempt me to
lug my carcase to kingdom come? I toss the
carrion cat, matted and stiff, into the incinerator, but I am
scratched, a little dark line to fester. My teeth
die first—I hone the stumps—and then the mastoid bone.
It will be enough, perhaps, if some nerve-ends remain
and a few circuits. The child's brain is a
vampire brain, with a little milk for oblivion,
suffering to see corruption. We have it all
between the eyes. Pale delicate throats invite us
to bed. Black widow with wings. The sun
lets down dark claws and bears
a bright hourglass on her belly. And I'll lie
torpid, glutted, a little trickle edging from the lips,
undead, with a rosy flush. Three aeons
and a million minds reverberate in my head,
in circles. Nobody wants to die. Nobody can live.
Eventually someone will drive the stake, with one
stroke cleave the neck. The net will rot, while the
garlic flowers.

Wood

With the first snow, the birches bend double.
The log sweats and burns, proving wood is
a little water and a little ashy earth but mostly
fire. My legs are stiff, the circulation
slow. I stand at the window.

Words for Some Songs

I. Ice Age

Thirty-five is, on the whole, a nice age,
But I can't stay here very long.
I look in the mirror and things are
just starting to go wrong,
And I know what's coming—an ice age.

So many things seem second nature,
Like the resilience in a good bone
Or the little springiness of the muscles
that they refer to as "tone"
—So many limbs in the way of a glacier.

But right now's not bad—don't remind me
Of the bland years I managed to wade through.
I burn much better now than I ever
did when I was twenty-two,
And the ice ahead is the same ice that's behind me.

II. Dream Song

My darling, last night as I lay on my bed,
I dreamt a long dream and in my dream you were dead,
In my dream you were dead.

I wept and I wept and my tears ran down
And an ocean formed where my tears hit the ground,
My tears hit the ground.

O I dreamt that I wept till that ocean was filled
And it flooded the forests and covered the hills,
It covered the hills.

And then it all flowed away and the hills were bare,
And when it was all gone the forests were there,
The forests were still there.

And I followed a funeral car where it led,
Or else I lay in that car instead,
I dreamt and I wasn't just sure who was dead.

And the earth was powdery, the ground was dry,
And a film of dust covered my eye,
Dust covered my eye.

My darling, that dream was dissolved in the dawn,
And waking I wondered why I was ever born,
Why was I ever born.

III.   Shopping Around

My love, when you go to the antique stores and
                            you bring back
Armloads of little knickknacks and assorted
                            bric-a-brac,
And you want my reactions to all your
                            new bought stuff,
I confess to you, my love, I've never loved anything
                            enough.

My love, when you come back from the supermarket,
                            your arms full
Of broccoli and Polish sausage and grapefruit and sauerkraut
                            and London broil,
And you wait for compliments because the salad's crisp and
                            the meat's not tough,
I do like your cooking, my love, but probably not
                            enough.

We both went to school, my love, to such a
                            lot of classes,
I learned a little from one old man, the
                            rest were asses,
And I wonder now how I managed to get through
                            all that stuff,
Loving a lot of things a little, my love, but nothing quite
                            enough.

My mother told me, my love, to love the Lord with
                    all my heart,
But the Lord and I tended somehow to drift
                    far apart,
Because it was just too hard to keep up that
                    lovely bluff
Without loving it, my love, at least not loving it
                    enough.

My love, the sun hits us from his bright spot
                    in the sky,
A common star, that burns as we do, and like us
                    has to die,
And whose hot glances play over a whole
                    world of stuff
That we couldn't hold on to, my love, even if we loved it all
                    and loved it all
                    enough.

IV. Last Things

A squirrel was mashed to death on South Main
           last Friday night,
And as might have been expected
He had to wait till Monday afternoon
                   with all the other litter
      [*newsprint, beer cans, garbage, old rubber, carrion, shite*]
To be collected.

I'd like to know, if such a thing could really
           be figured right,
When the last thing goes wrong with me,
What will just go on lying around,
                   and what of all I've known
      [*songs, filing cabinets, words, one or two ideas, a soft
      touch, sunlight, wood, mud, corridors, traffic noises, dead
      squirrels, shite*]
Will get buried along with me.

If you look around, the people that you see
           by day or night
All have proper expressions in the proper places,
But when they're swept up in the big sweep
                   along with the other waste
      [*wallpaper, stumps, dead squirrels, electric blankets,
      ashtrays, butts, post offices, societies for the prevention of,
      stamp collections, bomb shelters, die Fragmente der
      Vorsokratiker, me, you, an incredible amount of shite*]
How will death do their faces?

V. Fall Song

I can't say for sure that I'll always love you,
I've started so many projects and finished so few,
It's less and less often now I open a book and read it through,
But we'll see.

I won't put up any parp about the infinite
Or argue from predestination that we couldn't ever quit,
It wouldn't do to swear we'll never get tired because I have to
    admit
It could be.

Knives break, comfortable rocking chairs get so they creak,
The air goes out of air-mattresses and canoes begin to leak,
The Sheik gets too old to do it any more—even the Son of the
    Sheik,
Eventually.

So we'll see, it could be that I'll come to need total rest,
Or walking past a foreign post office find I've forgotten your
    address,
But on the other hand there's really very little to be said for
    emptiness,
So yes,
Let's just see.

And if you want to know what I think, remember what I told
    you,
All these doubts are a bill of goods I wouldn't want to have
    sold you,
I think I may die not grabbing for life so much as just groaning
    to hold you
One more season.